This Book Belongs to

_____

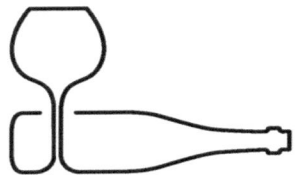

Wines are like fingerprints—every one is unique.

There is a science and art to wine that brings people together and enhances every experience. There is nothing like enjoying girl talk, date night, or even some "me" time over a glass or bottle of wine. With more than 11,000 wineries in the United States, how could you resist drinking wine.

If you were like me, I started out drinking only the sweet wines. Moscato was my thing, and you couldn't tell me anything. Over the years, my palate has matured. To learn wine is to taste wine and I tasted everything. I enjoy trying new wines with friends or just being by myself reading a book. I sipped for fun at first, then I became a wine guide with Traveling Vineyard. This sparked my interest and I wanted to learn more. I then expanded my wine knowledge and became WSET 1 and 2 certified. I am now in the process of creating my own wine brand. So where do you begin?

This journal will hopefully expand your knowledge of wine. You will learn tips for wine tasting, basic fruit flavors, serving temperatures, and food pairings. I want you to write down every wine that you taste, the food, the experience, and the company. So, grab a bottle and a pen. Start with one of the activities and let's begin your wine journey.

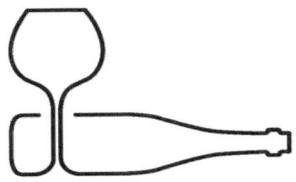

Wine Tasting Tips

See – Hold the glass by the stem and observe the different shades of color. White wines gain color as they age, while red wines lose color. Observe the legs of the wine; that is how slowly or fast the wine falls on the side of the glass

Swirl – Swirling is integral to aerate the wine and allow oxygen to "open it up."

Smell – Our senses of taste and smell are very directly tied. So, when you take a good long sniff of something, it will affect how you taste that something in the same moment. With most wines you will smell fruits and herbs. You may also smell wood, dirt, and spices.

Sip – Hold the wine in your mouth for about 3 seconds before swallowing. This ensures that the wine hits all parts of the tongue and mouth. You can gauge sweetness, acidity, bitterness, tannins of the wine.

Wine Terms

Acidity provides crisp and refreshing components to the wine; mouthwatering sensation

Aeration is introducing air/ oxygen to the wine to release aromas and flavors

Body is how thick or thin the wine is; mouth feel

Claret is the British name for red wines of Bordeaux France

Corky a term used if wine has a musty, moldy or cardboard smell caused by defective cork

Decanting is slowly pouring wine from the bottle to another container without disturbing the sediment

Dry is the term used to describe little or no residual sugar in the wine

Earthy a term used to describe an aroma of soil or dirt

Effervescence are the bubbles in sparkling wine

Oaky is a term used to indicate that wine has been fermented or aged in oak barrels; adds aromas and flavors of vanilla and baking spices to the wine

Tannin is the structure or backbone component of red wine; leaves bitter flavor or mouth drying sensation

Vintage is the year in which grapes are harvested for wine

Yeast is a microorganism that converts grape sugars into alcohol

Serving Temperatures

Sweet wine
Well chilled 43-46F

Sparkling wine
Well chilled 43-46F

Light to medium bodied white wine/ Rose
Chilled 45-50F

Full bodied white wine
Lightly chilled 50-55F

Light bodied red wine
Lightly chilled/ room temperature 55 – 64F

Medium to full bodied red wine
Room temperature 59 – 64F

Food & Wine Pairing

Have you ever enjoyed a wine and a food and didn't know why? Usually, the wine and food pairing has more to do with the experience and the people you are with. Some people go by region: what grows together goes together. Some people go by colors red wines go with beef and white wines go with salads and seafood. I always say eat and drink what you like regardless of what anyone says. If you like it, I love it! Use the table below to help guide you.

If Food is....	Wine will seem......
Sweet	Less sweet/ fruity and more acidic and drying/ bitter
Umani	Less sweet/ fruity and more acidic and drying/ bitter
Salty	More sweet/ fruity and less acidic and drying/ bitter
Acidic	More sweet/ fruity and less acidic and drying/ bitter
Fatty/ oily	Less acidic
Hot/ spicy	Hot and alcohol will be more noticeable

Wine o'Clock Coloring Page

Aromas and Flavor Profile

Floral	honeysuckle, blossom, rose, jasmine, hibiscus, lavender
Red fruit	Strawberry, watermelon, raspberry, cherry, cranberry
Black fruit	Plum, blackberry, blueberry, black currant
Citrus/ green fruit	Lemon, lime, apple, pear, grapefruit
Stone/ tropical fruit	Apricot, mango, melon, peach, banana, pineapple, lychee
Spice	Pepper, cinnamon, clove, nutmeg, vanilla
Herbs	Grass, green pepper, mint, rosemary, eucalyptus
Oak	Buttery, cedar, toast, nuts, coffee, chocolate
Earth	Leather, tobacco, mushroom, leaves, soil, dirt

White Wine Family

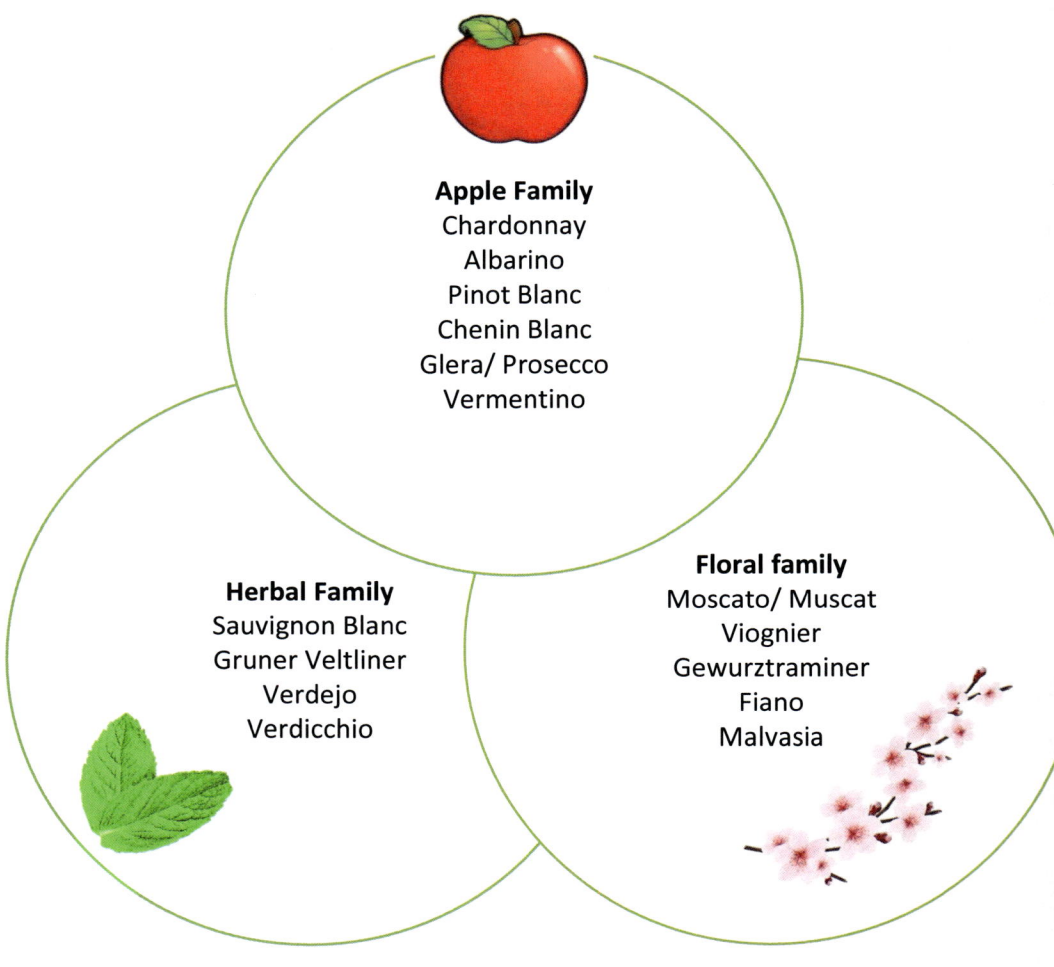

Apple Family
Chardonnay
Albarino
Pinot Blanc
Chenin Blanc
Glera/ Prosecco
Vermentino

Herbal Family
Sauvignon Blanc
Gruner Veltliner
Verdejo
Verdicchio

Floral family
Moscato/ Muscat
Viognier
Gewurztraminer
Fiano
Malvasia

Red Wine Family

Black fruit family
Cabernet Sauvignon
Merlot
Tempranillo
Barbera
Carmenere
Montepulciano
Corvina
Petite Sirah

Spiced fruit family
Syrah/ Shiraz
Aglianico
Monastrell/ Mourvedre
Nero D'Avola
Negro Amaro
Pinotage

Red Berry family
Pinot Noir
Dolcetto
Gamay

If you were a wine, what type of wine would you be and why?

_____
_____
_____
_____
_____
_____
_____
_____
_____
_____
_____
_____

Place wine label here

Name_____

Region_____

Grape Variety_____

ABV % _____   Price_____

See_____

Smell_____

_____

_____

Sip_____

_____

_____

Body	light	medium	full
Sweetness	dry	semi-dry	sweet
Acidity	low	medium	high
Tannins	low	medium	high

Paired with

_____

_____

_____

Comments

_____

_____

_____

_____

Overall rating   1   2   3   4   5

Buy again?   Sip   or   Sink

Place wine label here

Name_____

Region_____

Grape Variety_____

ABV % _____   Price_____

See_____

Smell_____

_____

_____

Sip_____

_____

_____

Body   light   medium   full
Sweetness   dry   semi-dry sweet
Acidity   low   medium   high
Tannins   low   medium   high

Paired with

_____

_____

_____

Comments

_____

_____

_____

Overall rating   1   2   3   4   5

Buy again?   Sip   or   Sink

Place wine label here

Name_____

Region_____

Grape Variety_____

ABV % _____   Price_____

See_____

Smell_____

_____

_____

Sip_____

_____

_____

Body	light	medium	full
Sweetness	dry	semi-dry	sweet
Acidity	low	medium	high
Tannins	low	medium	high

Paired with

_____

_____

_____

Comments

_____

_____

_____

Overall rating   1   2   3   4   5

Buy again?   Sip   or   Sink

Place wine label here

Name_____

Region_____

Grape Variety_____

ABV % _____   Price_____

See_____

Smell_____

_____

_____

Sip_____

_____

_____

Body	light	medium	full
Sweetness	dry	semi-dry	sweet
Acidity	low	medium	high
Tannins	low	medium	high

Paired with

_____

_____

_____

Comments

_____

_____

_____

Overall rating   1   2   3   4   5

Buy again?   Sip   or   Sink

Place wine label here

Name_____

Region_____

Grape Variety_____

ABV % _____   Price_____

See_____

Smell_____

_____

_____

Sip_____

_____

_____

Body	light	medium	full
Sweetness	dry	semi-dry	sweet
Acidity	low	medium	high
Tannins	low	medium	high

Paired with

_____

_____

_____

Comments

_____

_____

_____

Overall rating   1   2   3   4   5

Buy again?   Sip   or   Sink

Place wine label here

Name_____

Region_____

Grape Variety_____

ABV % _____   Price_____

See_____

Smell_____

_____

_____

Sip_____

_____

_____

Body	light	medium	full
Sweetness	dry	semi-dry	sweet
Acidity	low	medium	high
Tannins	low	medium	high

Paired with

_____

_____

_____

Comments

_____

_____

_____

Overall rating   1   2   3   4   5

Buy again?   Sip   or   Sink

Place wine label here

Name_____

Region_____

Grape Variety_____

ABV % _____   Price_____

See_____

Smell_____

_____

_____

Sip_____

_____

_____

Body	light	medium	full
Sweetness	dry	semi-dry	sweet
Acidity	low	medium	high
Tannins	low	medium	high

Paired with

_____

_____

_____

Comments

_____

_____

_____

Overall rating   1   2   3   4   5

Buy again?   Sip   or   Sink

Place wine label here

Name_____

Region_____

Grape Variety_____

ABV % _____   Price_____

See_____

Smell_____

_____

_____

Sip_____

_____

_____

Body	light	medium	full
Sweetness	dry	semi-dry	sweet
Acidity	low	medium	high
Tannins	low	medium	high

Paired with

_____

_____

_____

Comments

_____

_____

_____

Overall rating   1   2   3   4   5

Buy again?   Sip   or   Sink

Place wine label here

Name_____

Region_____

Grape Variety_____

ABV % _____   Price_____

See_____

Smell_____

_____

_____

Sip_____

_____

_____

Body   light   medium   full
Sweetness   dry   semi-dry   sweet
Acidity   low   medium   high
Tannins   low   medium   high

Paired with

_____

_____

_____

Comments

_____

_____

_____

Overall rating   1   2   3   4   5

Buy again?   Sip   or   Sink

Place wine label here

Name_____

Region_____

Grape Variety_____

ABV % _____   Price_____

See_____

Smell_____

_____

_____

Sip_____

_____

_____

Body	light	medium	full
Sweetness	dry	semi-dry	sweet
Acidity	low	medium	high
Tannins	low	medium	high

Paired with

_____

_____

_____

Comments

_____

_____

_____

Overall rating   1   2   3   4   5

Buy again?   Sip   or   Sink

Place wine label here

Name_____

Region_____

Grape Variety_____

ABV % _____   Price_____

See_____

Smell_____

_____

_____

Sip_____

_____

_____

Body	light	medium	full
Sweetness	dry	semi-dry	sweet
Acidity	low	medium	high
Tannins	low	medium	high

Paired with

_____

_____

_____

Comments

_____

_____

_____

Overall rating   1   2   3   4   5

Buy again?   Sip   or   Sink

Place wine label here

Name_____

Region_____

Grape Variety_____

ABV % _____   Price_____

See_____

Smell_____

_____

_____

Sip_____

_____

_____

Body	light	medium	full
Sweetness	dry	semi-dry	sweet
Acidity	low	medium	high
Tannins	low	medium	high

Paired with

_____

_____

_____

Comments

_____

_____

_____

Overall rating   1   2   3   4   5

Buy again?   Sip   or   Sink

Place wine label here

Name_____

Region_____

Grape Variety_____

ABV % _____   Price_____

See_____

Smell_____

_____

_____

Sip_____

_____

_____

Body   light   medium   full
Sweetness   dry   semi-dry   sweet
Acidity   low   medium   high
Tannins   low   medium   high

Paired with

_____

_____

_____

Comments

_____

_____

_____

Overall rating   1   2   3   4   5

Buy again?   Sip   or   Sink

Place wine label here

Name_____

Region_____

Grape Variety_____

ABV % _____   Price_____

See_____

Smell_____

_____

_____

Sip_____

_____

_____

Body	light	medium	full
Sweetness	dry	semi-dry	sweet
Acidity	low	medium	high
Tannins	low	medium	high

Paired with

_____

_____

_____

Comments

_____

_____

_____

Overall rating   1   2   3   4   5

Buy again?   Sip   or   Sink

Place wine label here

Name_____

Region_____

Grape Variety_____

ABV % _____   Price_____

See_____

Smell_____
_____
_____

Sip_____
_____
_____

Body	light	medium	full
Sweetness	dry	semi-dry	sweet
Acidity	low	medium	high
Tannins	low	medium	high

Paired with
_____
_____
_____

Comments
_____
_____
_____

Overall rating   1   2   3   4   5

Buy again?   Sip   or   Sink

Books and bottles coloring page

Read Between the Wines

Think about your favorite book. The characters in the book bring you into their lives and evoke certain feelings. Wine does the same thing. What type of wine pairs with the book you are reading?

_____   _____

Book   Wine

_____   _____

Book   Wine

_____   _____

Book   Wine

_____   _____

Book   Wine

_____   _____

Book   Wine

_____   _____

Book   Wine

_____   _____

Book   Wine

_____   _____

Book   Wine

Let's Play Wine-O BINGO!
How many wines have you tried?

Cabernet Sauvignon	Merlot	Syrah	Champagne	Pinot Noir
Riesling	Tempranillo	Bordeaux	Moscato	Sancerre
Chenin Blanc	Gruner Veltliner	Pinotage	Sauvignon Blanc	Grenache
Cinsault	Chardonnay	Rose	Gewurztraminer	Malbec
Pinot Grigio	Barbaresco	Viognier	Sangiovese	Zinfandel

Liquid Therapy

Self-Care is essential for your well-being. How do you relax? List some ways below then color the picture.

_____
_____
_____
_____
_____

Place wine label here

Name_____

Region_____

Grape Variety_____

ABV % _____   Price_____

Appearance_____

Smell_____

_____

_____

Taste_____

_____

_____

Body	light	medium	full
Sweetness	dry	semi-dry	sweet
Acidity	low	medium	high
Tannins	low	medium	high

Paired with

_____

_____

_____

Comments

_____

_____

_____

Overall rating   1   2   3   4   5

Buy again?   Sip   or   Sink

Place wine label here

Name_____

Region_____

Grape Variety_____

ABV % _____   Price_____

See_____

Smell_____

_____

_____

Sip_____

_____

_____

_____

Body	light	medium	full
Sweetness	dry	semi-dry	sweet
Acidity	low	medium	high
Tannins	low	medium	high

Paired with

_____

_____

_____

Comments

_____

_____

_____

Overall rating   1   2   3   4   5

Buy again?   Sip   or   Sink

Place wine label here

Name_____

Region_____

Grape Variety_____

ABV % _____   Price_____

See_____

Smell_____

_____

_____

Sip_____

_____

_____

Body	light	medium	full
Sweetness	dry	semi-dry	sweet
Acidity	low	medium	high
Tannins	low	medium	high

Paired with

_____

_____

_____

Comments

_____

_____

_____

Overall rating   1   2   3   4   5

Buy again?   Sip   or   Sink

Place wine label here

Name_____

Region_____

Grape Variety_____

ABV % _____   Price_____

See_____

Smell_____

_____

_____

Sip_____

_____

_____

Body	light	medium	full
Sweetness	dry	semi-dry	sweet
Acidity	low	medium	high
Tannins	low	medium	high

Paired with

_____

_____

_____

Comments

_____

_____

_____

Overall rating   1   2   3   4   5

Buy again?   Sip   or   Sink

Place wine label here

Name_____

Region_____

Grape Variety_____

ABV % _____   Price_____

See_____

Smell_____

_____

_____

Sip_____

_____

_____

Body	light	medium	full
Sweetness	dry	semi-dry	sweet
Acidity	low	medium	high
Tannins	low	medium	high

Paired with

_____

_____

_____

Comments

_____

_____

_____

Overall rating   1   2   3   4   5

Buy again?   Sip   or   Sink

Place wine label here

Name_____

Region_____

Grape Variety_____

ABV % _____   Price_____

See_____

Smell_____

_____

_____

Sip_____

_____

_____

Body	light	medium	full
Sweetness	dry	semi-dry	sweet
Acidity	low	medium	high
Tannins	low	medium	high

Paired with

_____

_____

_____

Comments

_____

_____

_____

Overall rating   1   2   3   4   5

Buy again?   Sip   or   Sink

Place wine label here

Name_____

Region_____

Grape Variety_____

ABV % _____   Price_____

See_____

Smell_____
_____
_____

Sip_____
_____
_____

Body	light	medium	full
Sweetness	dry	semi-dry	sweet
Acidity	low	medium	high
Tannins	low	medium	high

Paired with
_____
_____
_____

Comments
_____
_____
_____

Overall rating   1   2   3   4   5

Buy again?   Sip   or   Sink

Place wine label here

Name_____

Region_____

Grape Variety_____

ABV % _____   Price_____

Appearance_____

Smell_____

_____

_____

Taste_____

_____

_____

Body	light	medium	full
Sweetness	dry	semi-dry	sweet
Acidity	low	medium	high
Tannins	low	medium	high

Paired with

_____

_____

_____

Comments

_____

_____

_____

Overall rating   1   2   3   4   5

Buy again?   Sip   or   Sink

Place wine label here

Name_____

Region_____

Grape Variety_____

ABV % _____   Price_____

See_____

Smell_____

_____

_____

Sip_____

_____

_____

Body	light	medium	full
Sweetness	dry	semi-dry	sweet
Acidity	low	medium	high
Tannins	low	medium	high

Paired with

_____

_____

_____

Comments

_____

_____

_____

Overall rating   1   2   3   4   5

Buy again?   Sip   or   Sink

Place wine label here

Name_____

Region_____

Grape Variety_____

ABV % _____   Price_____

See_____

Smell_____

_____

_____

Sip_____

_____

_____

Body	light	medium	full
Sweetness	dry	semi-dry	sweet
Acidity	low	medium	high
Tannins	low	medium	high

Paired with

_____

_____

_____

Comments

_____

_____

_____

Overall rating   1   2   3   4   5

Buy again?   Sip   or   Sink

Wine Word Search

Find the wine varietals in the puzzle and label
which are red and which are white.

G	E	W	U	R	Z	T	R	A	M	I	N	E	R	U	Z	U	X	N
G	N	P	R	O	S	E	C	C	O	D	T	O	S	Q	L	R	M	O
S	P	R	W	J	X	K	T	P	N	Q	H	A	X	U	U	U	Y	N
C	I	U	Z	U	B	M	I	U	R	R	U	M	A	L	B	E	C	G
A	N	H	D	K	Y	N	A	P	J	V	W	N	P	U	J	N	Q	I
V	O	I	L	Q	O	I	B	Y	I	N	P	S	E	U	V	E	O	V
A	T	E	R	T	S	A	N	G	I	O	V	E	S	E	Z	T	T	U
X	N	T	G	I	F	N	N	D	M	C	C	U	X	L	A	P	T	A
K	O	R	B	V	E	O	W	U	N	V	K	L	Q	C	S	E	E	S
T	I	E	T	P	N	S	G	A	B	P	I	O	S	H	U	H	M	T
S	R	E	Z	B	C	V	L	S	H	W	F	O	N	R	C	I	P	E
Y	L	I	L	H	Y	B	I	I	E	A	M	A	E	A	P	H	R	N
R	I	A	C	Y	N	P	F	O	N	M	J	Q	N	G	T	B	A	R
E	N	M	O	I	S	G	D	K	G	G	I	E	B	O	H	F	N	E
C	C	G	N	A	Y	T	A	C	O	N	R	L	L	K	T	D	I	B
K	L	E	D	N	A	F	N	I	Z	G	I	R	L	L	C	D	L	A
H	H	L	S	C	J	S	Y	R	A	H	E	E	E	O	E	B	L	C
C	P	J	O	Z	N	K	J	U	J	M	R	E	R	Z	N	K	O	R
W	A	B	M	C	H	A	R	D	O	N	N	A	Y	Z	A	G	Y	B

_R_ Cabernet Sauvignon

____Chardonnay

____Chenin Blanc

____Gewurztraminer

____Grenache

____Malbec

____Merlot

____Pinot Noir

____Pinot Grigio

____Riesling

____Sangiovese

____Semillon

____Tempranillo

____Viognier

____Zinfandel

____Sauvignon Blanc

____Moscato

____Prosecco

____Syrah

____Cava

Wine Alphabet Game

Name something wine related that starts with each letter in the alphabet. How many can you get on the first try?

A_____   N_____

B_____   O_____

C_____   P_____

D_____   Q_____

E_____   R_____

F_____   S_____

G_____   T_____

H_____   U_____

I_____   V_____

J_____   W_____

K_____   X_____

L_____   Y_____

M_____   Z_____

Scavenger Hunt

How many items can you find in the room in 1 minute?

Wine Glass

Wine bottle

Corkscrew

Book

Candle

Coaster

Grapes

Cheese board

Wine stopper

Wine Scrabble

How many words can you make with
the phrase: "Wine Therapy"

_____
_____
_____
_____
_____
_____
_____
_____
_____
_____
_____
_____
_____
_____
_____
_____
_____
_____
_____
_____

Place wine label here

Name_____

Region_____

Grape Variety_____

ABV % _____   Price_____

See_____

Smell_____

_____

_____

Sip_____

_____

_____

Body	light	medium	full
Sweetness	dry	semi-dry	sweet
Acidity	low	medium	high
Tannins	low	medium	high

Paired with

_____

_____

_____

Comments

_____

_____

_____

Overall rating   1   2   3   4   5

Buy again?   Sip   or   Sink

Place wine label here

Name_____

Region_____

Grape Variety_____

ABV % _____   Price_____

See_____

Smell_____

_____

_____

Sip_____

_____

_____

Body	light	medium	full
Sweetness	dry	semi-dry	sweet
Acidity	low	medium	high
Tannins	low	medium	high

Paired with

_____

_____

_____

Comments

_____

_____

_____

Overall rating   1   2   3   4   5

Buy again?   Sip   or   Sink

Place wine label here

Name_____

Region_____

Grape Variety_____

ABV % _____   Price_____

See_____

Smell_____

_____

_____

_____

Sip_____

_____

_____

Body	light	medium	full
Sweetness	dry	semi-dry	sweet
Acidity	low	medium	high
Tannins	low	medium	high

Paired with

_____

_____

_____

Comments

_____

_____

_____

Overall rating   1   2   3   4   5

Buy again?   Sip   or   Sink

Place wine label here

Name_____

Region_____

Grape Variety_____

ABV % _____   Price_____

See_____

Smell_____

_____

_____

_____

Sip_____

_____

_____

Body	light	medium	full
Sweetness	dry	semi-dry	sweet
Acidity	low	medium	high
Tannins	low	medium	high

Paired with

_____

_____

_____

Comments

_____

_____

_____

Overall rating   1   2   3   4   5

Buy again?   Sip   or   Sink

Place wine label here

Name_____

Region_____

Grape Variety_____

ABV % _____   Price_____

See_____

Smell_____

_____

_____

Sip_____

_____

_____

Body	light	medium	full
Sweetness	dry	semi-dry	sweet
Acidity	low	medium	high
Tannins	low	medium	high

Paired with

_____

_____

_____

Comments

_____

_____

_____

Overall rating   1   2   3   4   5

Buy again?   Sip   or   Sink

Place wine label here

Name_____

Region_____

Grape Variety_____

ABV % _____   Price_____

See_____

Smell_____

_____

_____

Sip_____

_____

_____

Body	light	medium	full
Sweetness	dry	semi-dry	sweet
Acidity	low	medium	high
Tannins	low	medium	high

Paired with

_____

_____

_____

Comments

_____

_____

_____

Overall rating   1   2   3   4   5

Buy again?   Sip   or   Sink

Place wine label here

Name_____

Region_____

Grape Variety_____

ABV % _____   Price_____

See_____

Smell_____
_____
_____

Sip_____
_____
_____

Body	light	medium	full
Sweetness	dry	semi-dry	sweet
Acidity	low	medium	high
Tannins	low	medium	high

Paired with
_____
_____
_____

Comments
_____
_____
_____

Overall rating   1   2   3   4   5

Buy again?   Sip   or   Sink

Place wine label here

Name_____

Region_____

Grape Variety_____

ABV % _____   Price_____

See_____

Smell_____

_____

_____

Sip_____

_____

_____

Body	light	medium	full
Sweetness	dry	semi-dry	sweet
Acidity	low	medium	high
Tannins	low	medium	high

Paired with

_____

_____

_____

Comments

_____

_____

_____

Overall rating   1   2   3   4   5

Buy again?   Sip   or   Sink

Place wine label here

Name_____

Region_____

Grape Variety_____

ABV % _____   Price_____

See_____

Smell_____

_____

_____

Sip_____

_____

_____

Body	light	medium	full
Sweetness	dry	semi-dry	sweet
Acidity	low	medium	high
Tannins	low	medium	high

Paired with

_____

_____

_____

Comments

_____

_____

_____

Overall rating   1   2   3   4   5

Buy again?   Sip   or   Sink

Place wine label here

Name_____

Region_____

Grape Variety_____

ABV % _____   Price_____

See_____

Smell_____

_____

_____

Sip_____

_____

_____

Body	light	medium	full
Sweetness	dry	semi-dry	sweet
Acidity	low	medium	high
Tannins	low	medium	high

Paired with

_____

_____

_____

Comments

_____

_____

_____

Overall rating   1   2   3   4   5

Buy again?   Sip   or   Sink

Place wine label here

Name_____

Region_____

Grape Variety_____

ABV % _____   Price_____

See_____

Smell_____

_____

_____

Sip_____

_____

_____

Body	light	medium	full
Sweetness	dry	semi-dry	sweet
Acidity	low	medium	high
Tannins	low	medium	high

Paired with

_____

_____

_____

Comments

_____

_____

_____

Overall rating   1   2   3   4   5

Buy again?   Sip   or   Sink

Wine Word Scramble

Ardncoayhn _____

Ortp _____

Nptio ggorii_____

Lerotm_____

Naizelnfd_____

Ption rino_____

Becalm_____

Inglrise_____

Hraegcne_____

Eors_____

Uinnasogv nlcab_____

Rahsy_____

Xadurobe_____

Urndbygu_____

Coeoprsc_____

Let the Good Times Flow Coloring Page

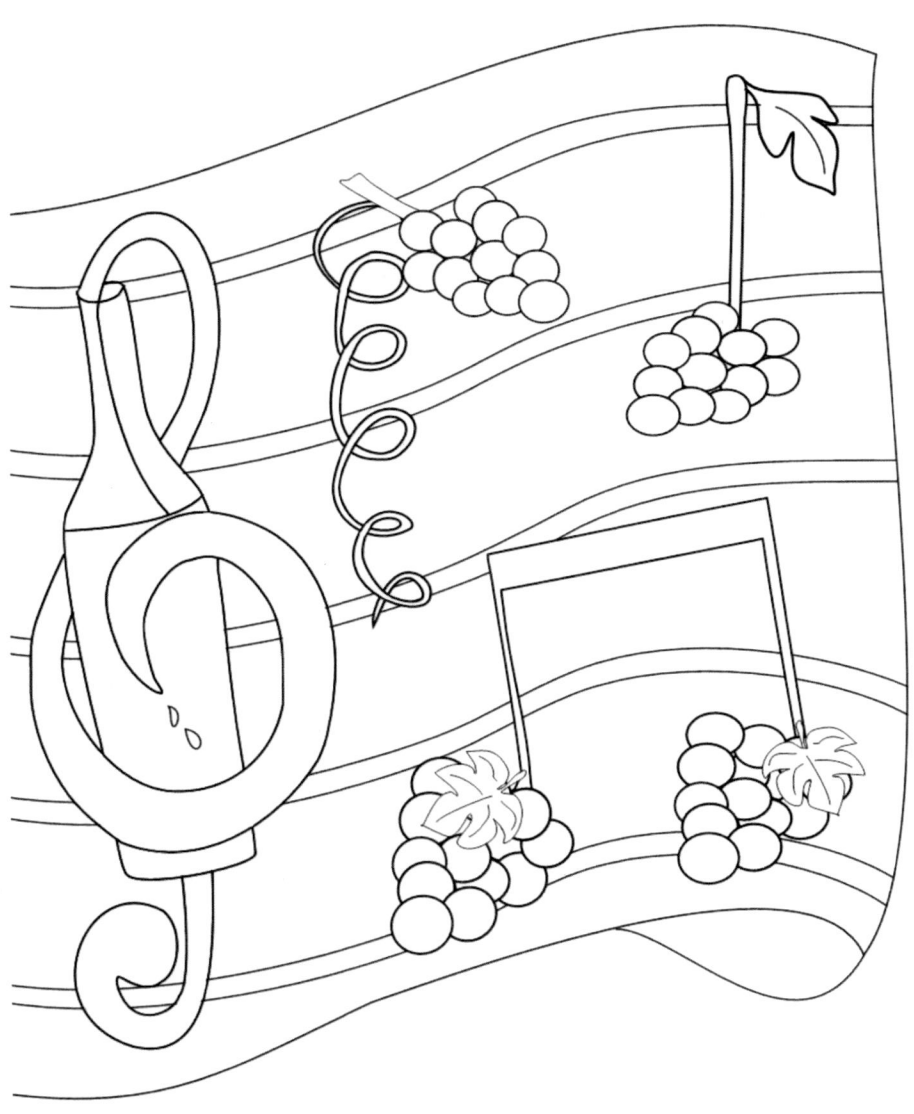

TV/ Movie and Wine Pairing

One of my favorite things to do is relax with a glass of wine in hand and sit on the couch to watch a TV show or movie. Finding the right bottle of wine to pair with the show can be difficult. Hopefully this guide will help you get started.

Comedy: needs something bubbly
Horror/Suspense: Sauvignon Blanc
Reality TV: Chardonnay
Romantic: Rose
Action: Pinot Noir
Documentaries: Syrah
Drama: Cabernet Sauvignon

_____

TV/ Movie   Wine

_____

TV/ Movie   Wine

_____

TV/ Movie   Wine

_____

TV/ Movie   Wine

_____

TV/ Movie   Wine

_____

TV/ Movie   Wine

Wine Directory/ Vineyards/ Wineries/ Shops

Wine Directory/ Vineyards/ Wineries/ Shops